Caring for New Christians

MARGARET ELLIS

WORD PUBLISHING
Milton Keynes, England

CARING FOR NEW CHRISTIANS

Originally published by Nelson Word Ltd. / Pioneer 1993.

This edition published 2000 by Word Publishing, 9 Holdom Avenue, Bletchley, Milton Keynes, Bucks, MK1 1QR, UK.

ISBN 1 86024 374 6

Designed and produced for Word Publishing by
Bookprint Creative Services, P.O. Box 827, BN21 3YJ, England.
Printed in Great Britain.

CONTENTS

ACKNOWLEDGEMENTS

I want to thank my husband, Roger, for his constant support, training and initiative ever since I was a teenager. He has always encouraged and released me to be the woman God has called me to be, and set me an unflagging example of service and sacrifice for the Kingdom of God.

I am sincerely grateful to my parents, Martin and Elizabeth Goldsmith, for the strong foundations they have built into me. And also to my sister, Ruth, for faithfully typing this manuscript and looking after Chloe.

I want to thank God for my little daughter Chloe who keeps me laughing all day and who is so easy-going in all I do. I am also deeply grateful to the many unseen people in the church who serve and support me with Chloe and the house, enabling me to continue in the things that God has called me to do.

Lastly, I want to give credit to Murray Jacobs, who first taught me and gave me the confidence to care for new believers in the church. Without these people I would be nowhere.

Margaret Ellis
April 1993

INTRODUCTION

Setting the Scene

The scene was set squarely 2,000 years ago by Jesus when He told the parable of the sower in Matthew 13. A farmer went out to sow his seed. But he found that the real yield was dependent on the environment in which that seed was nurtured. As Jesus called His disciples to be those workers who would bring in a mature harvest of followers of a living King, He began to show them what this environment would involve.

For myself the scene was set in our own church on the south coast of England where we found ourselves encouraged by a steady flow of new people finding faith in Jesus. When we began our first new congregation a few miles down the road, I was asked to take over the leadership of a course that we ran for new Christians, since the appointed leader was going off to begin a new church. In this way I started to get my hands dirty with what really happened to the people who responded to our appeals or became Christians by other routes. I must confess that there were times when what I had thought was an encouraging church-growth situation intensely discouraged me. I saw many of our new believers disappear through the back door as fast as they had come in the front. The writings that follow are therefore the culmination of my own musings, my searching of Scripture and of God's heart for the babies of our church family, whom I had grown to love and sorrow over. The practices that have emerged are a result of our failures as much as our successes.

Jesus clearly called us to make disciples, not just new converts (Matt. 28:19–20). We need to question 'test-tube' evangelism that nurtures growth outside the life of the body, and instead allow the different ministries within the church to build a womb together that will bring life to maturity.

It is dangerous in church to think that the gifts of pastors and evangelists are poles apart. This perpetuates a compartmentalised church life which increases the chances of people getting lost on the way from one department to the next: a bit like trying to get the right form out of the DHSS! In fact, the Bible encourages a much more holistic model of the body of Christ in which the different ministries flow together, each adding their own contribution, but each, in truth, being meaningless without the other. In the pages that follow, we will endeavour to build up a picture of what that womb should consist of.

As we look at what is involved in the miracle of salvation, we discover that the Bible uses various tenses to describe it. A story might illustrate this. A young Salvation Army evangelist was witnessing to people on a train one hot summer afternoon. Next to her in the carriage sat a vicar in a neat grey suit. Deciding to presume nothing, she took the direct approach and asked, 'Are you saved?' The answer she got successfully shut her up, if nothing else! The vicar replied, 'Do you mean: am I saved, am I being saved, or will I be saved?'

Of course he was right! In Ephesians 2:5 we see salvation as *an initial and completed act* which God has accomplished for those who have put their faith in Him. In 1 Corinthians 1:18 Paul adds to this another dimension which reveals that we are also *in the process of being saved*. We recognise this too as we look at our own personal lives and see ourselves increasingly growing into all that Christ offers us. However, we also know in ourselves that this is incomplete as we strain towards that perfection which we long for. So 1 Peter 1:5 speaks of a salvation that is *still to be fully revealed* at the end of time.

As we apply these three aspects of salvation to our care for new Christians (and for that matter also for older ones), we realise that it is inadequate to sit back and rejoice that new life has been born. Instead, we need a theology of salvation which motivates us in a very 'hands-on' way to encourage new believers to grow into maturity. Some may question if this is interfering with something that should happen mysteriously, or naturally, as the Holy Spirit does His work. Clearly, we would not wish to deny in any way the power of the Holy Spirit. Working supernaturally, He brings out the fruit of salvation. However, we need to hold together our understanding of the power of God with our understanding of our own role as partners with the Holy Spirit. While God is sovereign and can work without us, in His grace He usually chooses to work with us. Those who have known the joys and problems of having a partner in a work situation will appreciate the challenge of being good partners for the Holy Spirit to work with!

If God longs for His people continually to grow in His salvation, why is it particularly important to focus on the first few months of that growth? What is so special about the early days after we become Christians? Educationalists and psychologists have highlighted the importance of the formative months and years of a baby's life in setting patterns for their future lives. I would like to argue that this very early stage is equally important for a new Christian, whatever their physical age.

Why? Firstly, in Matthew 7:24–27 Jesus talks about the wise and foolish builders. The message is simple and clear: the foundations on which we build our lives are all-important when it comes to withstanding the pressures that will beat against us. We want to help new Christians build good foundations, avoiding a false satisfaction in fast but superficial outward growth. Such foundations have to be built and not presumed upon. It is interesting to note Jesus' description of a good foundation:

> 'Everyone who hears these words of mine and puts them into practice is like a wise man who built his house on the rock' (v. 24).

It is hearing which is put into practice—knowledge which is applied—that will build good foundations. Foundations are very difficult to lay once the house is up!

Secondly, we realise how important this initial stage is when we ask the question 'What are people born into?' Being the mother of a young child, I am particularly aware of the value of a healthy birth. All the way through labour the doctors and nurses were monitoring Chloe's heartbeat to check for distress and to aid a smooth birth. As soon as she was born they picked her up and put her to my breast so that she could nuzzle into me. Medical practice understands the importance of the environment through which and into which a baby arrives. If our new Christians can be born into a healthy, loving and believing environment, it will set a pattern that will enable them much more easily to grow into strong disciples. Roger Forster, speaking on the subject of motivating the church to evangelism, said:

> 'What people learn in the first few months of their Christian life is what they are likely to be in the rest of their Christian life, short of an explosion to blow them up! Therefore, what they hear and the environment they

meet within the church when they first arrive
is vitally important.'

The assets of a good birth must not be
underestimated!

Thirdly, as we care for new Christians we are
particularly aware of the displeasure of the enemy at
having lost one of his number and therefore of his
desire to snatch them back. Like a wolf prowling
around the sheepfold, it is always easier to pick out the
weaker sheep. Or, to use Jesus' analogy: the plant with
shallow roots is easier to pull out of the ground. We
have a particular responsibility towards the weaker
members of the body of Christ to protect them in their
vulnerability, and in the meantime to strengthen their
roots so that they are less easily plucked out by the
enemy.

Lastly, I would like to return to the parable of the
sower. It is easy to use this parable almost as an excuse
or as consolation for losing people. Have you ever
heard it said, fatalistically, when a prime new believer
falls away from their faith, 'Well, the Bible told us this
would happen!'—as if this makes it all right? The aim
of this short book will be to take Jesus' parable and to
use it positively to find both the heart and the strategy
to avoid losing those seeds. We want to get them
planted in such fertile soil that we will see a bumper
crop of radical, fervent, trained and equipped disciples
of Jesus Christ who can see the Great Commission
fulfilled! We want to fight for nothing less.

CHAPTER 1

IDENTIFYING OUR OBJECTIVES

My husband and I are useless at making decisions when we have a day off. If we are going out for lunch we will invariably wait until we are not only in the car, but also headed down the road, before one of us will venture to ask, 'Where shall we go?' What normally ensues is a circular meander around town which gets us nowhere, until one of us manages to force our brain into our mouth and make an appetising decision as to where to eat.

In looking after new Christians we need to avoid the meandering approach. This chapter will identify some of the objectives we should aim for as we aid new believers in their first steps of salvation. Knowing our objectives will help us to steer new Christians onto the main road, and away from blind alleys. For instance, I have known some to drown in their own questions! Identifying which are the key areas of theology they need to understand will enable us to steer them off worrying about the eschatological significance of a duck they found in Leviticus!

Prayer is focused when we know our objectives. So, too, we will find our practical energies focused. It is not that we aim to squeeze the new believer into our pre-arranged agenda. Of course, they will also be initiating the agenda as the Holy Spirit convicts them of different areas in their lifestyle and impacts them with God's life and love. However, in all their ferment of new life, we should not be passively drifting along simply being friendly. Hit-and-miss pastoring, largely dictated by their sense of priorities, is not our aim! Continually we need to ask the questions, 'Where does God want to take this person? And how are we to help them get there?' The rest of this chapter considers the answers under four main objectives.

1: Understanding of God's word and truth

The seed sown along the path in the parable of the sower is snatched away by birds. Why? Jesus explains:

> 'When anyone hears the message about the kingdom and *does not understand it*, the evil one comes and snatches away what was sown in his heart' (Matt. 13:19, emphasis mine).

Similarly:

> 'The one who received the seed that fell on good soil is the man who hears the word *and understands it*' (v. 23, emphasis mine).

God's word—His truth—lays a fundamental foundation for living out a relationship with Him. How does it do this? It opens windows into God's character, helping us to get to know Him more intimately. His word sanctifies us. It gives us moral parameters. The holiness that results not only leads to happiness, but also prevents us from falling away from Him. Sin is a major cause of casualties to new Christians! His word provides us with answers and wisdom that soothe the worries of life. His word breeds faith. It is the strong substance behind faith.

In a post-Christian society, the problem that confronts us is that many new Christians are ignorant of Christian truth. So we have to start from scratch.

Going round the circle of bright-eyed faces on the first evening of our Foundation Course for new believers, I ask them to explain what it is that they particularly want to get out of the course. One after another say that they want to understand what has happened to them in becoming a Christian: 'We want to understand the things we've experienced.' And so the questions start to flow.

Where to start

The best place to start is at the beginning. So we begin with salvation. Despite hearing a 'gospel message' and responding to it, it can be surprising how little of the gospel people remember. Please don't take it personally if you were the one giving the talk! The fact is that salvation is the work of God. While the talk was going on, the blindness over people's eyes was being removed, faith released, awareness of sin brought from the background to the foreground. The preaching was successful, but they may remember little of it!

Consequently, we need to lay the foundations of teaching about salvation. How did it happen? What is a Christian? It is important that new believers understand this because often when they talk with other Christians they are unsure if they are the same as them. What part has God played in their salvation and why? The fact that God has taken the initiative, reached out to us and paid the price, provides a whole new dimension of security to a new believer unsure of the strength of their own decision.

Once this has been emphasised, we can look at our side of the relationship. What do we do to clinch the deal? Teaching can then follow: on faith, repentance, confession, using our wills, honouring God. In looking at our side of salvation, make sure that you are preaching grace. Unintentionally, it is easy to slip into imposing good works and law.

The old has gone. The new has come. Presumably that is exciting! But what we really want to know is: what on earth is this new creation? It can be slightly unsettling to feel different inside, but not to know what that new substance is made of. Through our teaching we need to help new believers grasp the amazing changes which have taken place within them. In all of this, assure new Christians that they are saved. Let them hear you say, 'You are a Christian'!

What else to cover
Then go on from explaining the initial impact of salvation to how we put it into practice. For instance, baptism needs to come onto the agenda. 'Repent and be baptised' is the chorus that runs through so much of the gospels. Baptism powerfully seals repentance. It gives new Christians, as well as their friends and family, something physical and tangible to hold on to as a sign of their conversion. Many will be nervous. Many will consider themselves 'not ready' to be baptised. Turn in your Bible to the story of Philip and the Ethiopian eunuch, or Paul with the gaoler's family. Gently persuade them that a degree in theology is not the qualification for baptism. Encourage new Christians to believe that all that is required is a turning from their old lives and the start of a relationship with Jesus.

I have also been astounded over the years at how many people have a fear of water. Putting together my knowledge of the devil's strategies against new believers, and my appreciation of the importance of baptism in sealing their salvation, I can only say that it makes me somewhat suspicious! The good news is that the perfect love of Jesus casts out fear.

I remember a very well-to-do lady on one of our

Foundation Courses. She had a multitude of questions about baptism that I never seemed to be able to answer fully. It turned out that for 35 years she had suffered from a fear of water. She never went swimming. Even in the shower she endeavoured to keep her head dry. It only got wet when her hair was really dirty! We gathered round, gently but firmly praying for her to be freed from this fear, and for the love of Jesus to take its place. I think she had a few practices in the shower before her baptism, but a few weeks later we baptised her in the sea. She told the watching crowd, after she came out of the water, how it was the first time in 35 years she had allowed her head to go under water. And more to the point, she had felt completely calm, despite the fairly large waves! You never can trust an English summer, but we can trust God! Do check out if a fear of water is holding people back.

At Ephesus, Paul found some disciples who, he discovered, had been baptised in water by John. However, when he asked them:

'Did you receive the Holy Spirit when you believed?' (Acts 19:2)

they replied bluntly:

'We have not even heard that there is a Holy Spirit!'

We do not want our new Christians to be saying this several years down the line. We need to teach them from Scripture about the Holy Spirit and then lay hands on them as Paul did, so that the Holy Spirit comes upon them.

When Paul placed his hand on them, the Holy Spirit came on them, and they spoke in tongues and prophesied (Acts 19:6).

Turning to the work of the Holy Spirit in our churches, we find this can be very confusing to new people! I remember a Spanish student who became a Christian one summer through coming to our meetings. Concerned to explain all that was going on, I sat next to her one meeting. I heard people speaking in tongues and so asked her if she had any questions. 'Yes,' she said. 'Could you repeat for me more slowly what they are saying? I can't follow English when it is so fast.'

Even when we think we have explained, people may not have understood! I spent half an hour on one occasion turning up Scriptures and explaining to a little group of new Christians all about the gift of tongues. When I had answered all their questions, I asked them if they would like to ask God for that gift. One of them was an elderly lady. She touched my arm gently and whispered, 'I'll leave it for the youngsters dearie . . . at my age I don't think I'll be needing to travel abroad for holidays!' We need God's help to teach in such a way that people will come away understanding His truth!

Glancing more briefly at other issues, we want also to lay the foundations of understanding on such important subjects as developing our personal relationship with God. What is God like? How can we get to know Him through the Bible? How do we understand the Bible? How do we pray? For most new Christians the thought of praying out loud is more scary than watching *Nightmare on Elm Street*! How do we handle relationships of all types? What does the Bible teach about the church?

Lastly, do mention the fact that Jesus is coming again; it does make quite a difference to how we approach life! I remember the look of shock on one young lad's face in our church when I told him that Jesus would come again some day!

So what is the key in all this teaching? The learning process will continue all of our Christian lives, so we do not need to worry about cramming to cover everything. What we do want is a simple, but correct, starting point on the fundamental issues of faith and lifestyle. We are putting up the scaffolding that will sustain a strong building and provide the framework on which future finer points and details can be hung.

How should we teach?
We find the answer to this question more easily when we remember that our aim is for our teaching to become a source of life within those who are learning. We should be encouraged to be creative in the way we impart knowledge. The aim is for your new Christians to grasp truth and live it out; it is not just to get it off your chest!

If you can use something visual to communicate your point, it is more likely to be remembered. Find a picture or an object, or even act out what you are saying. For example, when teaching on baptism, you might explain that it is like an outward seal on our inward faith. It is like circumcision was to Abraham, 'a seal of the righteousness that he had by faith' (Romans 4:11). Take an envelope and a letter, explaining that the letter represents you, and the envelope, Christ. As you place the letter in the envelope, show how in conversion we are placed in Christ. However, whilst it is not entirely necessary to seal the envelope, it is pretty foolish not to. That's like baptism. It seals your conversion and makes you feel secure. A simple demonstration of this with a letter and an envelope will make an impression in a way that you are unlikely to achieve through an eloquent, but nevertheless theoretical, verbal communication.

As you teach, encourage new believers to turn up the verses in the Bible themselves. We want to show them physically that all our teaching comes from the Bible. It also provides them with good practice in finding their way around this massive book.

Personal examples of truth found in Scripture will help bridge the gap between the written page and our everyday lives. Be as honest and practical as you can, trying to find examples that will be relevant to them.

Ask questions too. Sometimes this helps those listening to engage their brains more and think through an answer. Skilful questions can often move you towards applying teaching to somebody's situation in a non-threatening way.

In all of this, ask yourself what will best relate to the person you are with. For example, how will you teach if they cannot read or write? Jesus managed it, and so can we!

2: Practical impact on lifestyle

He stared out of the window, his body tense with the turmoil of his mind. 'I know it is wrong to see her. The last thing I want is to split up anybody's marriage. But I can't live without her.'

*   *   *

'Welcome,' I said, smiling and sitting down beside a young woman, a newcomer to the church. 'We are really looking forward to having you as part of our church family. What do you do? Are you looking after the children full time or do you go out to work?'

'I work nights,' she replied carefully. She hoped the conversation would end there, but these church people seemed so interested in everything.

Then the question came again, 'What do you do?'

She looked her questioner straight in the eye, calculating her audience. In a level voice she replied, 'I'm a car thief. It works better at nights, and anyway, the children are asleep then!'

*   *   *

Here were two new people to the church. What would be the impact on their lifestyle of having become friends of Jesus?

The Old Testament word for 'hearing' carries with it the sense that true hearing always involves doing. You could not have heard if you did not do something about it. All the knowledge and understanding that we identified as our first objective is not supposed to stop at the brain! We are aiming to see 'fruit' produced.

The Bible is very clear, if not blunt, on the importance of this point. Examples of the nature of this fruit vary: at times it is described as attitudes (e.g. patience), at other times it is behaviour (e.g. honesty). But the message is loud and clear:

> Faith by itself, if it is not accompanied by action, is dead . . . a person is justified by what he does and not by faith alone (James 2:17, 24).

'Produce fruit in keeping with repentance,' cries out John the Baptist. 'Every tree that does not produce good fruit will be cut down.'

New Christians need help in applying their faith to their lives and allowing it to change them. At times it can be very complicated! In *Living God's Way* (Kingsway, 1984) Arthur Wallis wrote:

> The pressing need of the first days of the

Christian life is teaching that relates to the
business of living God's way in an alien
society.

So, we need to encourage and aid the practical
outworking of faith in lifestyle. However, as we do this,
it is vital to remember two things.

First, everything cannot change at once! Salvation,
we agreed, is a process. If God can save some parts up
for later, so can we!

A lady became a Christian through her teenage
son. Her marriage was on its last legs. For many years
an affair had been going on between her husband and a
younger woman. They barely spoke to each other, let
alone communicated. She said they lost their love for
each other many years ago. A healed marriage
overnight would be unreal. But a hint of 'fruit' started
to show.

'I feel I need to forgive my husband,' she confided
in me one day. It was not easy for her to say, but she
did. And so we talked through what that forgiveness
would involve and how she could find it. To be honest,
she was still riddled with other bad attitudes and bad
practices. It was a small drop in a large ocean. But it is
those drops that demonstrate that new life is within,
and it is those drops that start a flow of life that in time
changes everything.

Allow people to blossom into fruit slowly, so long
as it is steadily! If no fruit is produced, then the life is
obviously not getting through. The sap is not reaching
the branches. But savour every piece of fruit you do
see, however small. It is the sign of new life! If you
spend more time appreciating the small signs of life
rather than worrying about what has not changed, then
you will be rewarded.

Second, remember that 'fruit' will be different for

each person. Keep a sense of humour and do not get too intense! I remember one guy announcing proudly, 'Now I know I am a Christian: I've cut down from ten pints of beer a night to six!' If many other members of our congregation had said they were drinking six pints a night, I would certainly not have been encouraged by the impact of holiness upon them! But for him, that was a good start!

For another girl, the practical impact on her lifestyle of having found Jesus was simply that she wanted to stay in one geographic location. Her lifestyle had been deliberately rootless as she tried to run away from herself. Now that God lived with her she could live with herself.

Don't squeeze people instantly into your cardboard box of how faith should be worked out. Remember, everything cannot change at once, and change may be different for each person. Nevertheless, the gospel is about living words. Faith without action is dead. In a context of humanity and reality, we are looking to see knowledge outworked in practice.

3: Becoming rooted in the church

I will always remember a poster that was around when I was a teenager. It was pretty corny, but very graphic. A lovely warm coal fire glowed in the centre. A few coals lay separate, scattered around on the edge of the grate. You did not expect them to be alight, but somehow the contrast of how black and dead they were seemed shocking. The caption underneath left nothing to your imagination!

LIKE COALS IN A FIRE,
WE GO OUT WITHOUT EACH OTHER.

It would win no awards for subtlety, but perhaps it might for truth.

God, the great Creator, kept an exciting secret for centuries. A fantastic mystery would one day be revealed. What could it be? Another Mount Sinai? A new light display in the heavens? A more up-to-the-minute version of a rainbow? And then, with a thunder clap and graves being rent open, as the Son of God smashed death and came back to life, it all started. Not stopping at rising from the dead, He rose into heaven and sat down at the right hand of His Father, clothed in majesty and honour. And then God's wonderful secret was revealed: the new body of Christ. A body that would transcend the ages and provide a home for God's children. A body that would be a powerful agent for the outpouring of the Kingdom of heaven on a dry earth. A body that would be a radiant bride to the King. The body of Christ: the church.

The rest of the pages of the New Testament are full of teaching about God's great mystery, the church. We need church. We were made to be a part of it. We are sent out from it. How can we live dynamically without it?

Therefore, it is imperative that an early objective in establishing new Christians should be to root them firmly in church. It will provide so much that will give them a strong foundation. How we acheive this objective will naturally vary from one individual to another. So, what follows is some general advice to get you going!

Firstly, you may need to convince them of their need for church in a positive way. Some people, usually for reasons of emotional hurt, prefer to be 'loners'. With love and sensitivity we need to get under the surface and help people to work through to a point where they can get excited about being part of church.

Then, for some, we need to help them 'break into'

the church. It may be that they really want to get involved, but do not know how to. Sometimes church life can be like a fast train that whizzes through the station, beeping its horn. The windows are full of noisy, clamouring people waving their flags and shouting. But how on earth does one get on?! Can your church seem like this to new people?

The only thing wrong with that train is that it needs a guard! We need people who will blow the whistle, slow the train down at the pick-up points and open the door. If we are going to give a really good service, we can even usher them to their seats and serve them refreshments!

For new Christians in our churches, this will involve things like opening doors for them socially. As church is made up of relationships, some simple socialising will be very helpful. I often get frustrated when I am invited back for coffee with a crowd from the church, only to discover that none of our new people are anywhere to be seen! Organise some invites!

Like the guard on the train, another thing you can do is to slow others down so that the new people can catch on. It may be a simple introduction. It may be explaining some of the things that are being announced. Often our notices presume that the audience has heard the background from previous weeks. Without that background we might as well be giving the notices in tongues! The problem is that what could have been a good opportunity for your new believers to get involved in an event is lost.

Part of your enabling them to get rooted in the church will also be teaching them how to build relationships themselves. They do not want always to be at the bottle-feeding stage. Encourage them to initiate, to phone people up, and to look out for the needs of others.

A young mum who became a Christian a few

months ago waited to talk to me after a meeting. A few months previously she had given birth to a baby who was critically ill. They were testing him for brain damage. Many thought he would die. I had received a call asking me if I would visit them in hospital. We tiptoed somewhat nervously into the special care unit, very unsure if it would be appropriate to pray as none of the staff were Christians. However, we did pray, and from that moment on the baby started to improve; a few days later they were both discharged from hospital.

We are preparing our evangelism for this summer at the moment. Lots of talk is buzzing around about what events we will lay on. And now the same woman is standing in front of me enthusiastically selling to me the idea of her organising an evangelistic disco for us all. I smile with pleasure: that's what we want to see!

We do not want new Christians to be on the fringe of the church for the next year! Opportunities will emerge naturally for some, enabling them to feel involved. For others, you may need to create those openings. Never let it be said that all the jobs are taken!

4: Being saved to serve

It strikes me as very 'non-pastoral', the way that Jesus called His disciples. They did not leave their nets and follow Him into a cosy little sanctuary. They were called immediately to follow and to serve.

A few years ago I achieved a small personal ambition and swam in Israel's Dead Sea. Oh me of little faith, I found it hard to believe that I would bob up and down like an inflated buoy! But I did! The problem with the Dead Sea is that it has no outlet.

The most healthy position for any Christian to be in is one of active giving. And this applies to new Christians too. Our aim is to release new believers to be active for God. Many of us have been influenced by models of professional church leadership where ministry is the preserve of the experts. These experts tend to be middle-aged, both physically and spiritually. The shadow cast by this model causes us to keep new believers inactive and away from the fray of training. I would like to suggest a different model.

Of course, we can only give that which we have already received. I am not suggesting that we push new believers out of their depth. 1 Timothy 3:6 warns us against this. However, I am suggesting that we build an environment that encourages new Christians to give away freely what they have received in Jesus, and to feel confident in doing so. They need to be encouraged that God has good works prepared for them. Nurture in them hearts that want to serve, hearts that are able to dream dreams for God, and that realise they are needed and significant. It may be something as simple as designing some publicity for an event or doing somebody's ironing, but the seed is there.

I asked one of our new Christians recently what it was that finally made her decide to give her life to Jesus. She explained, 'It was the church playscheme that I worked on which helped me to decide that God was using me and could do more if I let Him.' The call to serve is a powerful and important root for Jesus' disciples, both then and today.

Use the following pages to jot down any ideas you have towards acheiving these objectives with new Christians you are caring for, or to note down progress made or problems encountered.

Notes

_____

_____

_____

_____

_____

_____

_____

_____

_____

_____

_____

_____

_____

_____

_____

_____

_____

_____

_____

_____

_____

_____

_____

_____

_____

_____

_____

_____

_____

_____

_____

_____

_____

_____

_____

_____

_____

_____

_____

_____

CHAPTER 2

LIFE THROUGH THE EYES OF A NEW CHRISTIAN

Think about all the people in your church and then think about their feet! Apart from the odd person trying to walk in a silly pair of stilettoes, most of them can walk and even run quite comfortably in what they are wearing. However, if we asked everybody to swap shoes with the person next to them and then try to run, we would have an altogether different situation!

So often we try to 'help' new Christians walk in our shoes and then wonder why they are moving so slowly and clumsily, tripping up as they go. Instead, we need to help them to walk from where they are at, and not presume to give them our shoes to walk in.

It is important that we stop and understand how life looks through the eyes of any individual new Christian we are caring for. The more we can understand, the more we will be able to take them on. This chapter offers many common traits that you should look out for and be sensitive to. They are all taken from real people and what they have said and been through. Of course, no two people are the same, and so what will be described can only be observations that will spur you on to a more particular understanding of those individuals that God gives to you. The key is that you allow yourself to be sensitised to what life looks like through the eyes of your new Christians.

Realising what is difficult

Everything we do has its own culture, and breaking into a new culture can be very difficult at first. What aspects of your church culture do new Christians find hard?

The Sunday meeting itself can be somewhat scary! Notice how new people often sit at the back, near the door! Some of the most difficult times can be before and after the meeting. Everybody else is busily talking to the scores of people they know, whilst the new Christians are wondering where on earth they can fit in.

There may also be occasions during the meeting when people feel left out or when they do not know what is going on. Someone from a small village Anglican church said:

> *'To begin with I felt very left out; everybody else knew who was delivering the prayers even though they had not been introduced. The sign of peace during a communion service was also totally alien, and I wondered what I should do.'*

Those who are contributing publicly to a meeting should be explaining constantly what is going on, so that all can feel included. Another new Christian from the same church said to me:

> *'A very simple guide to church terminology and services would have been helpful.'*

Continuing the conversation she explained how she saw it:

> *'The church is still very much a mystery to anyone who doesn't go to church—perhaps more advertising and a higher profile in the community*

*would help people who felt excluded by its
exclusiveness.'*

What explanations need to be given in your
meetings? If they do not come from the front, then sit
by your new Christians and whisper in their ears what
they need to hear.

Another thing that nearly all new Christians find
very difficult is if they are expected to pray out loud.
We don't often divide into small groups in our meetings
to pray, but it does sometimes happen. On one occasion
I walked around to check that all the groups were
getting on all right. I found a little group of new
Christians huddled together at the back and so decided
to join them. As I sat down they breathed a corporate
sigh of relief and said, 'Thank goodness you're here—
you can do all the praying!' Instead I took five minutes
to teach them how to pray out loud: 'Talk the same way
as you would to a friend, but just stick a 'Dear God' at
the beginning, try to cut out any swear words, and
when you dry up, even if it's mid-sentence, say 'Amen'
and then someone else will take over! If it is only short,
that's even better as it will save us all getting bored—
including God!' And with that they were off, and in fact
we had a really good time of prayer. But we need to
realise what is difficult and give them the support they
need.

Others are not used to keeping time and
appointments. A filofax-run church culture is alien to
them, and so remembering to turn up at a certain time
in a certain place just does not happen. You may need
to find them a couple of hours before the meeting and
then let them wander along with you.

For some, going to the house of someone they
don't know makes them feel very uncomfortable. Many
people have never even been to the homes of their best
friends at work. Remember what life looks like through

their eyes, and meet them in the position they are in.

Appreciating areas of insecurity

Sarah:

> *'I think I can honestly say that on becoming a Christian, I felt for the first time I had a future and something secure to hold on to. At the same time I felt a bit vulnerable as God had me in tears a lot of the time.'*

Bob:

> *'The most exciting thing for me as a new Christian was the knowledge that God was real, that He loved me and that, unlike humans, He would never let me down. A relationship with a caring Father represented for me a permanent security—a security which I had longed for. However, waking up the morning after I had made a formal commitment to God I realised that my life would no longer be the same—there was no turning back! The knowledge that I had handed over total control of my life to the Lord left me feeling slightly helpless: I was no longer in control. I was aware of the fact that God's plan for my life may vary from my own, and this left me feeling anxious.'*

New Christians often experience a mixture of feelings of great joy and security, coupled with feelings of anxiety or insecurity. There are so many changes going on, which on the one hand is incredibly exciting, but on the other hand is somewhat nerve-racking.

A common area of insecurity is the feeling of not

knowing enough. A guy who became a Christian one month before said to me:

> *'I feel as if I have a lot to learn without knowing where to start.'*

Another older woman said:

> *'I find it very difficult knowing the right thing to say in certain situations. People do seem to think that if you're a Christian you must know all the answers.'*

This sense of lack of knowledge can create feelings of insecurity for new believers when in the company of older Christians who seem to know everything! As a result, the more down-to-earth we can be, the better. It can also lead to feelings of insecurity when new Christians come to talking about their faith to their non-Christian friends. Whilst new Christians can be our best evangelists, as they have large networks of unsaved friends, they also very much need our support in this. For instance, in their enthusiasm they can be somewhat untactful! As one man said to me:

> *'As a new Christian I found it difficult to contain my enthusiasm about Christianity. My family and friends thought I had become a "religious fanatic". It was only with time that I realised that there are more subtle and convincing methods of expounding God's love than ramming it constantly down everyone's throat!'*

It would be far better to let them learn from our mistakes rather than their own.

We can also offer support on an emotional level as well as an intellectual level of knowing how to answer difficult questions. As I talk to new Christians, most of them express the difficulties they feel emotionally in telling people about their faith:

> *'I found it hard sharing my faith with non-Christians—would they think I was trying to be superior? Would they reject me?'*

> *'I felt terrified that I'd actually agreed to stand up in front of my family and friends and admit to my faith. It probably took me a month to get up the courage to tell anyone.'*

Many also express a concern about not knowing the answers to their questions:

> *'I found it difficult at first to tell friends and to a certain extent some members of my family. I felt I would be ridiculed and needed to know more, so as to answer the barrage of questions.'*

When we understand this, we can give a lot of vital support both in terms of emotional encouragement, and by equipping new Christians with answers and books that we have found will meet the 'barrage of questions'.

Being prepared for instability

'Prepare for the worst, but believe for the best' might be a good motto for those caring for new Christians. Some come to Jesus with such a clarity and determination that there is no looking back. However, others take a more bumpy ride into the Kingdom. As we have seen, there are many changes that take place and the effect of these changes can be very challenging. As a result, some new

Christians can be quite unstable in their new faith until they get their foundations sorted out. We get lulled into a false sense of security when one minute they are on a honeymoon high and then the next minute they are plummeting out of fellowship because of something that has happened. How should we respond to this as carers of new Christians?

Above all, we need to be prepared in our own emotions. It is easy for those who are caring for new Christians to be so disappointed at the first downward spiral that they give up, and then have to put all their energies into coping with their own discouragement. The enemy is on to a winner when we succumb to this classic tactic! Instead we need, in a positive way, to be prepared for the worst. In many ways, it is normal for a new Christian to go up and down in their faith for the first few months. We should avoid getting too intense about this!

However, it does mean that we have to be fast in catching them and halting that downward spiral. It makes it vital that we see them regularly to talk, so that we don't find such a deep spiral that it becomes too difficult to unwind.

All of the above traits are common to many new Christians. I hope this chapter has helped you to be more sensitive to their needs and feelings, which are often very different from those of more long-standing members of the church. What does life look like through the eyes of your new Christians? Use the following pages to note down any observations you make in this area from your own experience.

Notes

_____

_____

_____

_____

_____

_____

_____

_____

_____

_____

_____

_____

_____

_____

_____

_____

_____

_____

_____

_____

_____

_____

_____

_____

_____

_____

_____

_____

_____

_____

_____

_____

_____

_____

_____

_____

_____

_____

_____

_____

_____

_____

_____

_____

_____

_____

_____

_____

_____

_____

_____

_____

_____

_____

_____

CHAPTER 3

PASTORAL CARE OF THE NEW CHRISTIAN

The fundamental theme of this book has been to respond to Jesus' call to make disciples and not just 'to get people saved'. Therefore, before we throw ourselves into the 'how-to' of pastoral care, it would be beneficial to stop and look at what is meant by the term 'disciple'.

Discipleship: a biblical background

Mathetes is the word used in Matthew 28:29 for 'disciple'. A person is called a *mathetes* when they bind themselves to someone else in order to acquire this person's practical and theoretical knowledge. In this situation, it refers to people who have heard the call of Jesus and joined themselves to Him. In the New Testament the word generally describes the relationship of a pupil (the *talmid*) to the rabbi. The pupil chooses to subordinate himself (only boys were accepted) to a rabbi. He follows the rabbi everywhere he goes, learning from him and above all, serving him. The pupil's obligation to serve is seen as a fundamental part of learning the Law. The goal is a complete knowledge of the Torah and the ability to practise it in every situation.

Jesus did not call His disciples to master traditional modes of conduct. Instead, He pointed them to the present dawning of the Kingdom of God (Luke 9:59–62). To be a disciple of Jesus was ultimately and immediately an eschatological calling to help in the service of the Kingdom. We see therefore differences as well as similarities between Jesus' mode of discipleship and that of the rabbis.

Looking more closely at the literal meaning of *mathetes* it means 'a learner'. It comes from the word *manthano* which is the verb 'to learn'. The root of them both, *math*, indicates 'thought accompanied by endeavour'. This sums up much of what being a disciple involves! Endeavour is trying to put the teaching into practice. The demand is not that we always succeed, but that we try!

Lastly, disciples are spoken of as imitators of their teachers. The word *mimeomai* is used, reminding us of our own word 'to mimic' (see 1 Thess. 1:6 and 2 Thess. 3:7, 9).

So, discipleship described the learning process, but it was a process which necessitated the disciple adopting the philosophy, practices and way of life of the teacher. It was impartation of lifestyle based on teaching. Or as Jesus puts it in Luke 6:40:

' . . . everyone who is fully trained will be like his teacher'.

Jesus is the master or teacher in the discipleship relationship. We are merely at times the vehicles or ambassadors of His teaching. It makes sense therefore to model and mimic how Jesus taught. So, how did He disciple people? A major piece of work could be produced answering this question. However, I want to draw out two keys that can guide us.

Firstly, Jesus shared His life with His disciples and taught them through His own example. So, the disciples must have observed Jesus many times withdrawing from the crowds and taking time to pray. Eventually, the penny dropped and they asked, 'Lord, teach us to pray.'

Secondly, He speaks into the immediate situation making His teaching very poignant. We see this in Luke 14. Large crowds flocked to hear Him. Many of them were probably only there for the simple reason that He was the only live entertainment in the neighbourhood. Into this environment He taught:

'If anyone comes to me and does not hate his
father and mother, he cannot be my disciple.'

It must have cut right into their hearts. It is often not until people are brave enough to speak directly into our situations that we really learn.

From Jesus' example we learn much about how to pastor a new Christian. Allow them to see into your personal life. Let them see how you cope with failure or how you chose a boyfriend. Let them quietly observe how you build intimacy with your Father in heaven. Let your own example be as much of a teacher as your mouth. Don't just talk together about trivia. As you get to know each other be honest and personal in a very natural way. If you become aware of areas in their lives where God could particularly help them, try and share with them incidents in your own life where you have found similar answers. As Roger Forster says, 'Christianity is caught rather than taught.'

Similarly, we learn much from Jesus' directness. Teach gently into people's immediate situations. Do not be afraid to speak out and give guidance that will provide an understanding of the ethics and principles of Scripture in a given situation. We are not to manipulate or tell people what to do. But we are right to point out the thistles that may choke the seed. At least then if they die, they have done so deliberately! The truth is, if we don't teach directly into the immediate situations as they come up, they will often turn into the thorns that choke people.

Friendship: the fundamental ingredient

We could not talk like this to someone in the street. So what gives us the right to speak like this with a new Christian? Inside and outside the church, rights come from relationship. Rights are given and won. To be in the position to do any of what we are talking about in this chapter, there must be a friendship between you and the new Christian. If you skip this paragraph, you may well come unstuck!

Friendship comes in a multitude of different shapes and sizes. Be encouraged! Where friendship was built before salvation, your job is easy. If this is not the case, get stuck in fast! Whether you become like a peer-group friend or more like a parent or big-sister figure, you must build friendship. It can be hard to make friends quickly with someone you don't know very well, but this is no time for bashfulness, rejection or insecurity!

Jesus trained His disciples in a very human way. They cooked together, travelled together and generally shared their lives. When He died, He asked John to take His place as a son to His mother. As a group they were all intimately involved in friendship.

I used to teach History in our local comprehensive school. When I walked into the classroom on a Monday morning, what I had thought and done over the weekend was irrelevant to my lesson and stayed at home. It is an accepted part of our education system that, as a teacher, my private life and my professional life have little interplay. Not that this would stop the kids endeavouring to indulge in as much gossip as they could glean!

A radically alternative form of teaching is modelled to us by Jesus. The challenge to all of us who have gone through a formal education system is to throw off this pattern and be transformed by a more biblical approach to learning: an approach which is rooted in relationship.

I listened sadly to a friend of mine as he talked. He is a vicar. He and his family had recently been moved into a new vicarage. He described to me the pros and cons of their new home. The good thing was that they had loads of space for the children; an advantage which was offset by the poor heating! With enthusiasm he then explained to me the brilliant design of his office. His parishioners could ring the bell on a side door and come through to his office without ever having to go through the main house. 'It will be wonderful for my wife and children,' he smiled, 'as they need never be disturbed.' Apparently, some bright architect had come up with this idea for vicarages many years ago.

I tried hard to smile, but inside I felt as if something was wrong. Is this really going to be the best context for those parishioners to grow into maturity as Christians? I just wondered if they might learn more from watching him play with his children and talking to his wife, and then having a quiet coffee with him in the kitchen. Jesus was a great friend to sinners, to children and to tax collectors. A cup of tea in Zaccheus' home enabled Him to talk to him about his business practices and led to a mini-revolution not only in that man's life but in the whole town.

The point is, many new Christians go through times of doubt or temptation after the 'honeymoon' period of their initial salvation. This is when the enemy can snatch away that seed from under the farmer's eye. If we can be alongside them as friends, holding their hands, we can carry them through these times. If we are slow, we wake up when it is all too late. If we are watchful, but with an inadequate relational bridge, they will also be in danger. We try to reach out to them, but the bridge collapses beneath us. Friendship is the greatest challenge and the greatest reward.

The rule of priorities

We took a young lad into our home soon after we were married. He had just become a Christian and, as he was effectively homeless, we figured the easiest way to look after him would be to have him live with us. He was only about eighteen months younger than me, but he was soon calling us Mum and Dad. Probably the greatest things we got out of it, apart from practice in bringing up a teenager, was that we became celebrities overnight in town! He was a street kid extraordinaire. If I went shopping with him, every young person we passed would bound up and say hello.

But the reality under his winsome character was that he was in a real mess. He had never known his father. His mum lived with a man he did not get on with so he was not really welcome there. We rapidly discovered that he had never been 'parented' in the basic skills of life.

We started to teach him to set an alarm and actually listen to it, so he could get to work on time and stop getting the sack. My husband, Roger, spent hours teaching him how to work out what money he had, and more to the point, what money he didn't have, so that we could try to reduce the number of debt collectors at our door! And then he started bringing home his pregnant ex-girlfriends for me to 'counsel'! If a list was being compiled, we could add to it his low self-image, his fear of the dark, his occult involvements, drinking too much, smoking the odd illegal substance as well as the legal stuff, and generally keeping us awake at night before our time!

Our young lodger may sound a bad case, but in many ways he is very normal!

Only yesterday, our new Christians were in the kingdom of darkness, and a lot of that old life will come with them. In the first chapter we discussed the important objective of seeing their new-found faith impact their lives at a practical level. But this cannot happen all at once. The question we are faced with is, 'Where do we start?'

I would like to suggest two approaches. First, we have to learn what are priorities. In the foregoing list, all the problems add to the mess, but some of them are less important. Ask God what the priorities are. Sometimes the priorities are like the roots behind a cluster of other problems. If you chop off the branches, more will sprout again because you have not pulled up the root. So, for the lad who lived with us, what caused him to sleep around and have a low self-image, which resulted in not going to work, was the insecurity he felt because his mother and father had never really loved him. As we loved him ourselves, prayed for him and taught him to receive the love of his heavenly Father, he became more able to overcome his weakness with women.

A worthwhile question to ask of any given problem is whether that issue is going to stop the person growing in God now, or whether it can wait. Where there are problems of all types in people's lives, they do cause a ceiling beyond which they will not be able to grow. However, particularly for new Christians, there may still be some sky between their heads and the ceiling! It is the sky of God's grace which has bought them some free time. It may be tomorrow's priority.

Secondly, in all these things, we must find God's timing. Notice how God picks His moment to put His finger on different areas of our lives. The problem may in fact have been there for a long time, but in His grace, our Father knows when we are ready. There are times with new Christians when we have to trust God to convict them. This does not mean that we should be afraid to teach, for instance, the principles of His morality on the same subject. But we can teach in a way that gives the new Christian a backdrop against which they can stand their own picture, rather than giving them the barrel of a gun to look down!

The rule of gentleness

When my daughter was one year old, God used her to teach me the fruit of the Holy Spirit. At that time patience and gentleness were obviously top of His priorities for me. I developed an eye for seeing what she was planning to destroy next! As a result, my constant job was to remove her from the next vase or precious object she was about to lunge at and sink her teeth into. She did not know any better so there was no point in being angry. The best approach was to be gentle but firm.

Much can be learned from this when pastoring new Christians. In many ways they too are only like new babies. When explaining things to them, be clear, do not fudge issues, but be gentle. Start with the subtle approach! They may not realise, for example, that something they are doing is not right. When my husband first became a Christian, he genuinely did not know that it was wrong to get drunk. Consequently he would turn up to church each Sunday morning with a splitting hangover from the night before. What made it worse was that often his long hair would be matted to his head where beer had been tipped over it the night before and he hadn't bothered to wash it!

His youth leader must have had a word of wisdom. In a very matter-of-fact way he approached Roger with a list of dates for their next meetings, and asked him if he might prepare a Bible study for the younger teenagers, giving a biblical view of alcohol. The thought of doing his first Bible study made him feel a bit nervous, but thinking that at least it would be familiar territory, he accepted. The youth leader thanked him and produced a list of verses that might help 'get him going' in his studying. In the privacy (if not quietness!) of his bedroom, his eyes started to pop out as he read verse after verse against drunkenness. His youth leader must have breathed a sigh of relief the next Sunday when Roger delivered a well-balanced talk on drinking in moderation, and the problems with drunkenness! What is more, his breath smelt of coffee. Subtlety is often the best policy!

Gentleness also means that we don't take authority. We don't have any! Our only authority is Scripture. Use the Bible, explain what it means, point out relevant sections and persuade. But never attempt to impinge on another person's free will. Part of growing up is learning to make the right decisions. Parents and others guide and inform. As we care for new Christians, this is our role. However, in our enthusiasm, we must never deny them the freedom to make their own decisions.

Lastly, we also need to apply the rule of gentleness as we pray with new Christians for their emotional needs. As more mature Christians, we may be used to praying with each other for healing in different areas of our emotions. It is wonderful to know a God who works in this way. However, we need to realise that much of our ability to receive God's healing is because, over the years, we have learned to trust His love and stand in faith against the things that come against us. There is an unseen framework that our prayers and counselling fall into. We cause a disturbance if we pour a litre of the best wine into a sherry glass. Far better just to give them a sherry glass full of the wine! I would suggest that the strength of our praying and counselling should be directly proportionate to the strength of the individual's unseen spiritual framework.

Do counsel and pray as emotional needs come to the surface. But be gentle and light in the way you do so. Don't go wading in with deep 'ministry' too soon, as they may not have the framework to contain it and live in the good of it afterwards. Unless there is a real crisis, we will probably be better off taking chips off the block for a while. Meanwhile we can be building a stronger framework for the future.

The rule of encouragement

This is a simple but enjoyable rule for pastoring new Christians. No one blossoms under disapproval, but we all flourish under encouragement. Encourage every first step, whether it is praying out loud for the first time, getting baptised, or telling a colleague that they have become a Christian. Where discouragement is faced, be alongside them, helping them to find hope in the situation. It may be facing the reality of a partner who is not yet saved. Or it may be the discouragement of our own flagging personalities. Whatever it is, find ways to encourage them that God is with them and will see them through.

Encourage new Christians too into all of the riches that are theirs in Christ. They don't have to sit like the polite child at the party, wide-eyed at all the glamorous food, but unable to choose what to take. Reach out and place in their hands the inheritance that is theirs: security as to where they are going when they die; a peace inside whatever the storms; fun and laughter.

Encourage endlessly. It's good news being a Christian!

The rule of prayer

What happens backstage is easy to forget, but without it the show wouldn't go on. We pastor people as much through our prayers as when we are with them. In every situation, the power of prayer is a tool given to you. In all of the good things we have looked at so far, without God's breath in them, they will be like paper houses. Pray for your new Christians, that God will give them understanding of His truth in such a way that the 'penny will drop'. Pray for moral strength for them in the pressures that they are under. Pray for protection from the evil one. Pray for blessing and joy to come on all they do. The devil will be fighting to snatch them away, but we can pray that they will stand firm.

Notes

_____

_____

_____

_____

_____

_____

_____

_____

_____

_____

_____

_____

_____

_____

_____

_____

_____

_____

_____

_____

_____

_____

_____

_____

_____

_____

_____

_____

_____

_____

_____

_____

_____

_____

_____

_____

_____

_____

CHAPTER 4

RUNNING A NEW CHRISTIANS COURSE

Having a focal point within the church for new believers is often very productive. It precipitates opportunities for them to ask questions and to get to know new people, as well as providing the church with an easy vehicle through which to care for new believers. Some sort of 'beginners course' can be a useful means of delivering this. Any such course must be adapted to the particular culture and needs of the new Christians within that group. To be most effective, it requires a flexibility and creativity on the part of the local church to form a vehicle that will best suit its own people. This chapter will provide ideas that have been tested in local churches on how to run a new Christians course. It is hoped that these ideas will stimulate other churches to add to and develop their own models in line with their own people groups.

The aim of a new Christians course is not to isolate them from the church, but rather to integrate them more fully into that body. The presence of a special group should not be perceived as taking over the full responsibility for those new Christians, but rather as an aid to everything else that is going on. Caring for new Christians needs to involve the whole church, not just some perceived specialists. It should be an attitude and a hallmark that pervades every area of church life. To put it in Roger Forster's words:

'Discipleship involves being bonded together

> in relationships, therefore it demands a
> church community. So to bring new
> Christians through to maturity (disciple) we
> must have a good alive church context to
> bring them into. Through this atmosphere
> the new Christian will 'catch' their calling
> and who they are to be in Christ.'

Our starting point therefore for any new Christians
group should be in the training of the whole church to
think and to care. The setting up of a special group will
be the natural extension of this hallmark.

How should we go about organising such a group?

Filling the course with people

At times, filling the course with people can be easier
said than done! Have you ever seen people saved, but
then barely seen them again?

Of course, there are many different reasons for this,
but I would suggest that friendship and personal
contact is the key to unlocking the problems. It is not
enough to stand up and make announcements at
meetings that any new Christians are invited to join a
course that is being run. Some will respond to this, but
many won't.

The whole church needs to be involved in taking
the hands of the new Christians that they know and
linking them in with the beginners course. This will
involve chatting with people as to what the course is
about and why they will enjoy it. Once persuaded (or
nearly persuaded!), they can then be personally
introduced to the leaders of the beginners group, and a
conversation can be initiated that will answer their

questions and calm any fears. It may even help if their friend comes with them to the first meeting or two until they get to know other people.

Where people have become Christians through evangelistic street work, or have wandered into a meeting having seen an advertisement in the paper, there may not be anybody in the church who knows them at all. In this case, our street evangelists, or whoever else was involved, need to be diligent in following them up themselves, or at least taking responsibility for handing them over to others. In our church at the moment we are experimenting with creating a whole team of 'befrienders' who will pick up such new Christians, enabling the evangelists to continue their work. We don't want our evangelists to lose their incentive to see people saved because they cannot cope with the follow-up!

The course leaders themselves also need to be outgoing to the new believers on a personal level, making contact with them and extending a personal invite to the group. If the church is large, the course leaders would do well to have buzzing lines of communication with the most productive evangelists. They may know of new Christians who are somehow unknown to everyone else. A good ear needs to be kept to the ground!

Well-communicated public notices must not be forgotten either. It is worth making a habit of profiling your new believers course whenever the gospel is preached. When this is done, please make it easy for a new Christian to find the relevant course leader afterwards! 'Speak to Mary in the blue jeans if you are interested,'—this is wholly inadequate if you don't know who Mary is!

The structure of the course

Structures vary greatly from church to church, but the following will provide food for thought.

When to meet?
One approach is to try to find a time in the week that is convenient for everybody. This has the advantage of being user-friendly, but many other disadvantages!

On a practical level, it usually turns out to be impossible to please everybody and in the process the group ends up with major confusion and headaches!

On a theoretical level, much is to be said for the idea of using the same night as your house-groups. Later on in this chapter we will look at the critical point of the hand-over from the beginners group to the main flow of your church activities, which in most churches will be some sort of house-group. It is at this point that new Christians can be vulnerable and even be lost to the church, falling between the two stools. If the new Christians have adapted their lifestyles to being free on the house-group night, they are more likely to find their way into that group. We are all creatures of habit, and once the routine is established, the transition into a house-group will happen much more easily.

How long should the course run?
Again, there are no right or wrong answers to this question, but there are factors to consider.

Some churches run very long courses of six months or even a year in length. The advantage of this is that the new Christians can be very well established. There is also no disruption to their environment as they are able to stay together until they are no longer new Christians!

The disadvantage of such a long course is partly in the danger of perpetuating a position of immaturity, whereas our aim is to encourage the process of maturity. It also separates the newer Christians from the rest of the church for rather a long time. Both the new Christians and the older Christians will lose from this separation.

A second problem in running such a long course is that of leadership. Our structures should reflect and facilitate our faith targets. If we are to have a continual stream of new believers into our churches then we need to provide groups that are regularly starting for them. Another vulnerable point at which we can lose people is the stage between them making a commitment to Jesus and becoming fully established in the church. We do not want new Christians hanging around in limbo for too long, unsure at what point they can relate to the church. If courses run for a long time, a lot of new leaders will be needed to cater for the demand. Less experienced leaders may have to be used.

In view of the above points, in our own situation we run a much shorter course, of about ten weeks only. We find that this gives enough time to cover the basics in our teaching, as well as to build a level of relationship with the people. However, they do not become so settled that it becomes hard to integrate them into a house-group.

We also find that some new Christians go through a cycle whereby for the first two to three months they are in something of a 'honeymoon period'. Hopefully they do not come down to earth with a bump, but there is a degree to which a different level of reality emerges. Again, we have found that at this point of 'change of rhythm' they can be slightly vulnerable. Consequently, we have found it to be much more productive to hand the new Christians over into the house-groups while they are still at the tail end of their honeymoon period. This way they still have the new energy to take the change positively, and hopefully, with the fresh challenge of a house-group, they will not notice the end of their honeymoon period.

Where to meet?

An obvious and effective meeting place is the home of one of the leaders of the group. This gives a great advantage to that leader in the type of 'friendship pastoring' discussed in the second chapter. Having got used to being in the leader's home for the meetings, the new believers are far more likely to feel comfortable enough to drop in at other times. It is interesting to note how hospitality is listed as an important part of leadership in 1 Timothy.

However, there is no harm in experimenting with different locations. If there is a group of new Christians who all live on a certain housing estate, for example, it may be preferable to take the course to them. This can be very effective evangelistically, although it depends on having a good host who is able to provide regular hospitality. Some churches have hired rooms off local pubs in which to hold their new Christians groups. This has the advantage of being neutral (and often familiar!) territory for people to come to. It also has the added bonus of allowing people to relax with a drink afterwards!

What size group?

'As big as possible' is of course the evangelistic answer to the above question. When we do get hundreds of people saved at one time we will have to run groups of 50 to 100 and simply have a lot of helpers so that the personal side isn't lost. When my parents were missionaries in Indonesia they had a rule that they would not baptise fewer than about 35 people at a time, as it would be a waste of the church's resources.

However, when simply faced with a regular trickle of new believers, we should probably look at a size of group that will squeeze into an average living room! Perhaps around eight to twelve people. The dynamics of a small group are very beneficial. It provides enough people for the quieter members not to feel exposed, but a good diversity of questions and interests that will help the meetings go with a swing. The sense of being part of a bigger group can be wonderful for new Christians. It provides a variety of people with whom they can identify and make friends, as well as encouraging them with the sense that they are not the only ones in their position.

These are the advantages of running a course with a small group size. However, the situation sometimes arises whereby there are only one or two individuals who have been recently converted, or where someone is unable to come to the group that is run. In this case a 'personal' course can also be very worthwhile. If there is literally only one new Christian, it is worth considering having two people involved in leading the course for them. A course that is 'one-to-one' can be rather intense and one-dimensional in perspective. Perhaps it could be run by a mature Christian along with a slightly younger Christian.

How often should we start courses?
Accepting that the regularity with which we can start courses will be dependent on demand, it is nevertheless helpful to think through our goals. Goals release faith and energy; we may just be surprised and attain them!

The most important question to consider is, 'What is the longest a new Christian will have to wait before they can start a course?' Ideally, it should not be much more than a month. Therefore, a good working goal would be to have two new beginners courses running all the time. One group would start as the other group was mid-way through its course. If there were enough leaders to run three different groups, they could have a few weeks off to rest and rally people for the next one!

The content of the course

Subjects for teaching

The criteria for choosing what subjects are relevant for a new believers course are firstly, that which is fundamental to doctrine for the early stages of faith and secondly, that which is of practical importance in strengthening new Christians in their relationship with God and His people.

The following are suggested outlines of the sort of subjects that can be covered. Any individual course may need to add a session on a particular subject that is of concern to that group, but may well not be generally applicable to other groups.

Session 1: General introductions to the course and each other. Teaching on the Father Heart of God.

Session 2: What God did . . . God's side of our salvation.
This would focus on the cross, the problem of sin and forgiveness.

Session 3: What you did . . . our side of becoming a Christian.
This would look at repentance, choosing for God, faith and receiving His forgiveness and Fathering.

Session 4: A new inheritance.
This would look at what our inheritance is in Christ. What is this new creation? It will

involve looking at aspects of our inheritance such as:

- freedom from guilt as well as sins that enslaved us;
- a new father and family;
- life after death;
- a new purpose in life.

Session 5: God's plan and how we fit in.

This would seek to give an overview of God's plan of redemption for mankind. Since the Fall, God has been outworking His plan to win back mankind to Himself and bring His Kingdom in. Our part is to work together with God to see His Kingdom extended all over the earth. Into this context, a flavour can be given as to what is involved in 'the Kingdom' and encouragement that the members of the group have an important part to play in God's plans.

Session 6: Baptism in water.

This would give thorough teaching on the meaning and significance of baptism, with the aim of convincing all the new believers of the need to be baptised themselves, as an outward demonstration of their inward new life.

Session 7: Baptism in the Holy Spirit.

Background teaching should be given on the person of the Holy Spirit before looking biblically at the baptism of the Holy Spirit, what difference it brings and how to receive it. However it is handled, it is important that this is followed up with an opportunity for people to be filled with the Holy Spirit.

Session 8: Talking to God and hearing from God

Two sessions can easily be made from this one! It looks at prayer: how to pray, when to pray and praying out loud.

'Hearing from God' can cover the different ways in which God speaks to us, but it is suggested that the main focus should be on reading the Bible. Hand-outs or books can be given out on why we can trust the reliability of Scripture. A practical framework can then be given as to how to understand the Bible and some ideas as to how to go about reading it.

Session 9: The church and relationships.

This session could be done through a combination of questionnaire and discussion, looking at the following questions:

- What is the church?
- What is the role of relationships in the church?
- How do we build good relationships?
- How do we handle relationships that go wrong?

This session is also a useful opportunity to let the members of the group talk about any difficulties they may have faced in these areas, as well as think through how they themselves can initiate and build new friendships in the church.

Session 10: Where do I go from here?
It is suggested that this last session gives personal encouragement and advice to the group as to how to go on with God from this point. In this context, the teaching can focus on the fact that Jesus is coming again and therefore we are called to be witnesses. How can we best share our faith with others?

Baptisms

It is very much to be recommended that baptisms are organised before the group ends, and therefore are seen as part of the course. Ideally, the opportunity to be baptised should be given about three weeks after the subject of baptism has been taught. This gives time for the new Christians to work through their feelings about being baptised and to invite family and friends.

If the baptism meeting is part of the course, the whole group can go together, giving each other moral support. Where there are members of the group who are not going to be baptised, for differing reasons, it is good for them nevertheless to be part of the event.

Social events

Organising a few social events for the group can be very helpful in developing relationships, as well as a lot of fun! Think through carefully what they would all enjoy. If there is a diversity of age groups or interests, it may be best to 'do' something together, rather than have an evening that depends on the conversation flowing.

Who should do the teaching?

It is more consistent to have one or two people who are good at teaching to lead most of the sessions, particularly for the first few weeks. This will presumably be the leader/s of the group. If the leader of the group is doing the teaching this enables the new Christians to get to know that leader, and establishes a security in the group.

However, for a few of the later sessions it can be beneficial to invite in 'guest speakers' to lead parts of the evening. A change of voice is usually refreshing and provides a greater breadth of perspective. This is also a strategic opportunity for the group to get to know some of the key people in the church, whether this is one of the main leaders, an evangelism team leader or a house-group leader.

How should the material be taught?

If our objective, of grounding new Christians in God's truth, is to be achieved then there should be plenty of reference to Scripture in all that is looked at. While we must avoid the extreme of losing the flow of the teaching in too much fluttering of paper, it is good to get the group turning up and reading a good number of verses themselves.

The opportunity to ask questions is another important part of the course. It may be helpful to stop and take questions at regular points through the teaching. Always leave an open-ended time at the end of the evening as well, for questions to be asked. Providing regular question times is a good way of containing red herrings that may otherwise disturb the communication of more important issues.

Teaching should be made fun and digestible! The

teacher's voice should be broken up regularly with other modes of communication, be this a clip from a video, a visual aid or a quick role-play. Interactive sections in the evening involving questionnaires, interviews and other types of group involvement greatly aid the digestion of the teaching. Relevant anecdotes bring the material alive and make it human. And of course humour is the best sugar to help the medicine go down!

Generally, in terms of the content of the evening, it is best to avoid any attempts at worship or group prayer. These are not a priority and are likely to over-stretch the embarrassment levels of the group! As they grow in confidence together, prayer can be introduced. Start by getting them to pray for each other in pairs, giving them lots of direction as to what to say. But it is probably more realistic, at least initially, to avoid expecting them to pray out loud in front of everybody.

The leadership team

What sort of leaders are we looking for?

A careful choice of leaders to run the new Christians course is vital. As this is one of the most important areas of growth and investment for the future in the church, we are wise to deploy quality leaders to head the group. New Christians are very impressionable, but far from stupid! This is probably not the place to train an untested new leader as the stakes are too high.

In these main leaders, we are looking for people who are able to teach and who have a good understanding of broad theological issues. They should be able to present a logical argument and care about the practical outworking of such arguments. They should also be able to spot a heresy at its early stages!

It is equally important that they are good at

building friendship and sensitive to what others are going through. They need to care about people, notice their needs and not be quite happy to forget someone who has withered in their faith.

The role of 'helpers'
Unless the group is very small, it will be impossible for one leader to build adequate relationships on a personal level with each new Christian. A small team is needed whose brief will be to give themselves entirely to the friendship side of caring for new Christians. They should be responsible for looking after a maximum of two to three people (if they are working or have other ongoing demands on their time it is unlikely that they will be able to care for more than this number of people effectively). These helpers do not need to be great theologians or teachers. They just need to be ordinary Christians who love the Lord Jesus and will give time to help the new Christians feel part of the church, and look out for their needs.

The helpers are the ones who should be giving the new Christians a lift to the meetings, sitting next to them and making sure that they are included in the conversation. The helpers can provide a great support to the leader/s by setting a good atmosphere while people are arriving, cracking a few jokes and generally picking up on the personal needs of individuals. This is not to say that the main leader/s will not also be building relationships with the members of the group, but it protects them from being spread too thinly.

If there are four or five 'helpers' in a group it may be unnecessary for them all to come to every meeting. We don't want too many older Christians around! As less mature leaders, it may also be better for them not to be taken completely out of their house-groups. A rota can be organised whereby they come every other week, going to their house-groups on alternate weeks.

An excellent bonus of such a 'helpers' system is the leadership training it provides. If the main leader monitors and supports them effectively they will learn a lot. However, this monitoring is crucial, as we cannot afford to trust them with responsibility, only to find a month later that little has been delivered. It is worthwhile defining with the helpers how often they should be meeting with their new Christians on a social level. Ideally this should be once a week, or at a minimum once a fortnight.

Fortnightly 'leaders' meetings' can then be held in which the helpers feed back on how they are getting on with their new Christians and on any particular issues which may be emerging. The leader can then teach them and advise on how to take each situation forward. If particular prayer or counselling is needed, the leader may need to be involved with the helper. In this way the helpers can learn their first lessons of pastoral care.

The leaders' meetings can also be used by the main leader to talk through expectations of the helpers, encourage them in what they are doing and point out things they may have forgotten. If the meeting does not end up in praying for each other, a good prayer time can then be had for the new Christians!

Having been trained in this way, many helpers will go on into other areas of responsibility in the church. A turnover of helpers through the years will mean that in a real way, many people in the church will have been trained in the care of new Christians.

Ending the group

The ending is as important as the beginning! The aim in everything is to see new Christians who will go on in God and in the church. The hand-over from the new believers group into the main flow of the church in house-groups is a critical last hurdle. The more that can be done to make this a smooth and easy progression, the better.

Decisions need to be made half-way through the new Christians course as to which house-group they will be going into. With three to four weeks to go, the house-group leaders can be introduced to the new Christians coming into their group. In these last three weeks the house-group leaders and members of the house-group should be initiating friendships with the new believers. By the time it comes to the first night of house-groups, the new believers should already feel at home with a lot of the group.

If the link needs to be strengthened even more, the 'helpers' can go with some of their people for the first night of their house-group, or until they feel settled.

In addition, the hand-over to house-groups should be bolstered by good communication with the house-group leaders so that they know what to expect. The house-group leaders can be under the false impression that because a person has been through the new Christians course, they have received teaching on every major issue! Similarly, the new Christians will feel more secure about going to a house-group if they know what to expect.

For the first month, the new Christians team should keep a watchful eye on how their people settle into their house-groups, picking up on any teething problems. After this they can be awarded some time to collapse before gearing up for the next group!

To conclude

The call to make disciples is a great one. There are lives in our hands that God is trusting us to care for. The parable of the sower was not given for us to be fatalistic, but to be forewarned and therefore forearmed. Let's rally our churches to take up the challenge—to see the seed that we sow fall on such good soil that it produces a crop, yielding 30, 60 or even 100 times what was sown.

Notes

_____

_____

_____

_____

_____

_____

_____

_____

_____

_____

_____

_____

_____

_____

_____

_____

_____

_____